PAMELA ROSE
Wild Women of Song

GREAT GAL COMPOSERS OF THE JAZZ ERA

Wild Women of *Song*

GREAT GAL COMPOSERS OF THE JAZZ ERA

by

PAMELA ROSE

Foreward by Rebeca Mauleón

THREE handed MEDIA

San Francisco

For my Sisters & Mother

PRINTED IN THE UNITED STATES OF AMERICA

Library of Congress Control Number 2011941330

ISBN 978-0-615-54855-5

Published by Three Handed Media
P. O. Box 590893
San Francisco, CA 94118-0893
(415) 386-0935

For more information about this project: www.wildwomenofsong.com

COVER & GRAPHIC DESIGN: Jennifer Melnick, Olio Arts

PHOTO ARCHIVIST: Farrol Mertes

10 9 8 7 6 5 4 3 2 1

Special discounts are available on quantity purchases by educational institutions,
associations, and others. For details, contact the publisher at the address above.

Orders by U.S. trade bookstores and wholesalers: Please contact author and publisher
at Tel: (415) 386-0935; www.wildwomenofsong.com; idacoxjazz@gmail.com.

TABLE OF CONTENTS

Alberta Hunter wrote a song called "**Remember My Name**" when she was 83 years old. One can't help but wonder if she wasn't imparting a significant truth: it's a terrible thing to be forgotten.

When I recorded my **Wild Women of Song: Great Gal Composers of the Jazz Era** CD in 2009, I thought it would be an interesting angle to arrange and interpret songs written by women from Golden Age of Jazz (1920 through 1950). But a funny thing started to happen. I realized that although the songs I was choosing were fairly well known standards, the songwriter's name (unless she had also been a singer) was often new to me. And yet some of these women composers and lyricists were quite prolific, with strings of hits to their names.

Why aren't the names Doris Fisher and Dorothy Fields as familiar to us as Harold Arlen or Johnny Mercer?

These were feisty, talented and determined women in the middle of the most thrilling era in American music. Alberta Hunter wrote a blues which heralded a seismic change in the music industry. Dorothy Fields summed up the Depression by writing "**I Can't Give You Anything But Love.**" Doris Fisher helped make stars out of Louis Prima, Pearl Bailey and Rita Hayworth.

It was a fascinating journey to collect the photos and anecdotes which became part of our touring show *Wild Women of Song*. Audiences often asked me for additional information, which led me to deepen my research and assemble these biographies and photos as a 'take home' guide to the show.

Most of these accomplished women seemed to have vanished from memory with barely a trace left behind. Perhaps this is because they didn't have adoring widows determined to burnish their legacies. Or they themselves were uncomfortable talking about their achievements later in their lives. Or maybe, we all have just succumbed to a sort of cultural amnesia which has erased the presence of, and importance of, women in the Jazz Era.

Sadly, none of these women are still living – but I was lucky enough to gain the help of some of their family members and friends to secure some hard-to-find images and personal insight into their lives and work habits. Of particular assistance were David Lahm, the son of Dorothy Fields, Katharine Weber, granddaughter to Kay Swift, Peter Mintun, and Harold Jacobs, who befriended Doris Fisher in her last years and rescued a trunk full of news clippings and photos from being thrown away upon her death.

This collection is not strictly limited to American Songbook writers, but also includes some key women who helped light the torch of what we think of as American music. The attitude and power of songs by Ida Cox and Lil Hardin Armstrong popularized a music conversation that informed many of the songs we call Jazz Standards. And for those who don't think the Blues has much to do with the Songbook, listen again to Gershwin. Or better yet, Peggy Lee.

The lives and times of these hardworking women songwriters, how they tiptoed around a minefield of cultural stereotypes while still fulfilling the drive within them to write, has been a subject that caught my heart. My earnest wish is to help us all 'remember their names,' while celebrating from a decidedly feminist angle the exciting, vibrant sounds of the Classic Jazz Era in American Music.

"It's easy to overlook a musician who usually ends up being a footnote in someone else's biography" – and thus begins a chapter in this much-needed anthropological study of the unsung heroines of jazz. What author, chanteuse and expert dramatist Pamela Rose imparts upon us is the all-important role of the griot – the designated storyteller of African tribal society charged with recounting a culture through oral history, song and more. Rose is the ideal ambassador of these women's stories because she is one of us: a living, breathing and blues-belting Wild Woman who has found her true calling as an advocate for those musical pioneers who were brushed under the rug, or mentioned only as footnotes in the male-centered world of jazz biography.

How can it be that well over a decade into the 21st century, women still struggle for equity in a music so deeply connected to generations of artists striving to have their voices heard? Jazz – America's classical music – is the product of the collective consciousness of those attempting to break through the rigidity of the Eurocentric musical cannon, and women were a part of that story as well. And yet here we are, waving our flag, tooting our horns (literally and figuratively) and hoping the stories of these amazing pioneers will not go unnoticed.

Wild Women of Song is more than a case study or collection of biographical data on women from a particular era in jazz. It is the equivalent of a manifesto on the extraordinary contributions of women composers, songwriters as well as interpreters, whose significance was often disregarded due to their association with male counterparts, many of whom whose careers skyrocketed precisely **because** of these women! Louis Armstrong would not have evolved as the musician he was if it were not for the mentoring, coaching and tutelage he received from his wife, the extraordinary pianist Lillian "Lil" Hardin. Kay Swift's clever, deft songwriting was put on hold for years while she aided George Gershwin during his most productive period.

Some of these women transformed their struggle for equality into meaningful change. For blues singer-songwriter Alberta Hunter, decades of effort finally allowed her to recoup her rightful royalties for the smash hit "**Down Hearted Blues**." Peggy Lee refused to be intimidated by Walt Disney, and won a landmark victory after a 15 year court battle over video rights to her own songs.

So we reflect on these truths and also honor the past by celebrating the women represented in this worthy tome. Might I also suggest we look around and witness the extraordinary women in our midst who are continuing to carve the path for the future Esperanza Spaldings of the world...whether or not the biographers of America's music will finally cast gender aside and value a musician for her or his talent and skills alone remains to be seen. We will continue to be strong and united self advocates!

- Rebeca Mauleón

Rebeca Mauleón is an acclaimed pianist, composer, arranger, author, educator and producer. Her composing credits include music for television, film, software and symphony orchestra as well as for artists such as Tito Puente, Carlos Santana, Joe Henderson and others. She is a Grammy-nominated producer, a tenured professor of music history, performance and composition, a contributing writer to National Geographic and Jazz Times Magazine, and is Director of Education for SFJAZZ.

International Sweethearts of Rhythm

ALBERTA HUNTER

1895 – 1984

Woman of the World

All Alberta Hunter wanted from life was to make $6 a week singing in Chicago. Tiny, homely and dirt poor at fourteen, she took advantage of a free train ticket from Memphis to Chicago, knowing no one there except the daughter of her mother's friend, for whom she had no address. Her indomitable spirit, which would lead her to become an international star, shattering race, gender and age barriers her entire life, carried her fearlessly forward on that train.

By some fortunate twist of fate, she got off the streetcar exactly where her one Chicago contact, Ellen Winston, lived. Ellen found Alberta a job peeling potatoes and a place to sleep. But sleep wasn't what young Alberta was after: night after night she prowled the streets, trying to gain entry into anywhere there was music. And in 1910 music cascaded out of every doorway. A new sound had migrated north from New Orleans: syncopated, rapid, inventive, joyous. Alberta finally managed to get a slot singing at a run-down joint called Dago Frank's. Looking back on those days, Alberta said that the prostitutes liked her because she was no competition, the johns felt sorry for her, and the tips inspired her to keep learning new songs, strengthen her voice (no microphones back then) and develop her own winning persona and style. Early on she grasped that every song had a message, and with her warm personality, hand on one hip, expressive face, and throaty, velvety voice, she delivered that message to a growing audience.

By 1915 she was so popular that songwriters paid Alberta to introduce their new tunes, knowing she could put a song over with an audience. She was one of the first to sing "**Sweet Georgia Brown**" for Maceo Pinkard, and W. C. Handy reverently handed her an ink-fresh "**St. Louis Blues.**"

In 1917 she headlined the Dreamland Ballroom, where she became the toast of Chicago, billed as "The Finest Singer in the West." People poured in to hear her. Al Jolson and Sophie Tucker were front and center, studying this petite dynamo with her particular blend of vaudeville and blues. Often she shared the bill with King Oliver's Creole Jazz Band, introducing Alberta to her fellow Memphisian Lil Hardin (soon to be Armstrong) with whom she developed a life-long friendship.

Alberta recorded for the first black-owned phonograph company, Black Swan, while she was trying to break onto Broadway in New York. She also recorded sides for Paramount Records, often with Fletcher Henderson, Fats Waller, and Louis Armstrong accompanying.

One day Alberta Hunter's good friend and pianist Lovie Austin heard Alberta humming and singing a tune over and over and thought it was so good, she encouraged Alberta to finish it. As Ms Hunter told biographer Frank C. Taylor, quoting Lovie:

"Ooh, that's wonderful honey." Lovie told her that this was a song that ought to be recorded. "Well, okay," Alberta told her, needing her help to write down the music. "If you think it could be a good song, you can have the tune that I'm humming, and I'll take the words." Lovie sent the manuscript of the music and lyrics to Washington, D.C. where they were copyrighted on April 25, 1922.

—Alberta Hunter: A Celebration in Blues, Frank C. Taylor

"**Down Hearted Blues**" became a huge hit. Alberta's own recording sold well, sheet music sales went sky high and people packed the clubs to hear her sing that song, so full of heartache and attitude. In 1923 Bessie Smith's recording of "**Down Hearted Blues**" sold 780,000 copies in six months, breaking all records and creating a run on gramophones. Yet all that Alberta Hunter received from that song back then was $368. Due to some legendary shady publishing practices of the era, it took her until 1948 to correct that particular wrong.

Replacing Bessie Smith in *How Come?* a show billed as "A Girlie Musical Darkomedy" in New York, Alberta stopped the show, bringing a star-studded opening audience to its feet. Smack in the middle of the Harlem Renaissance, Alberta loved those thrilling days of the Cotton Club, Langston Hughes poetry readings and a booming economy that finally allowed room for even Negroes to move up in society and the arts. From 1923 to 1927 she reigned supreme, but longed for wider horizons.

Unlike many of the women in this book, Alberta married only once, and briefly, in 1926. This had much to do with her independence of spirit but probably an equal amount to do with the fact that Alberta preferred women to men. Lesbian, gay, and bisexual musicians were not uncommon in the jazz community - Billy Strayhorn and Bessie Smith being the best-known examples - but sexuality was considered a private affair and Alberta never spoke publicly about her romantic life.

Upon hearing of the success of Bricktop and Josephine Baker in the clubs of Paris, Alberta sailed to France. Working steadily on the vibrant Paris club circuit, Alberta thrived on the wide open embrace France gave to African-American artists, welcomed as beautiful, exotic and cherished guests, so different from the treatment received in the States.

During an appearance in England in 1928, she was noticed by Oscar Hammerstein, who was scouting for a British production of his musical *Show Boat*. She became an international star playing the part of Queenie, singing **"Can't Help Lovin' Dat Man of Mine"** to the profoundly beautiful and talented Paul Robeson night after night. Even King George V came to Drury Lane as an enthusiastic fan.

Alberta returned to America right after the great Crash to find vaudeville dead and black artists fairly shut out of Hollywood. Always longing to work and travel, she put together a cabaret act that toured from

Stockholm to Cairo. During and after World War II she travelled the globe ceaselessly as the USO's first black act.

Following the death of her beloved mother in 1954, and feeling a waning appreciation for her style of music, Alberta decided to retire and apply for nursing school at age 62 (although she lied and said she was 50). Few of her co-workers or patients at Goldwater Memorial Hospital in New York City were aware that she had been an internationally renowned singer and songwriter.

However, Alberta Hunter had not been entirely forgotten by the music world. Record producer Chris Albertson pulled her out of retirement in 1961 to record with Victoria Spivey and Lucille Hegamin. **Songs We Taught Your Mother** was such a success, she was invited to record again, this time reuniting her with Lovie Austin and Lil Armstrong. She loved nursing, and never missed a day of work in 20 years, when she was forced to retire at the age of '70' (although she was actually 82 years old).

But the most endearing and perhaps enduring legacy of Alberta Hunter was yet to come. An encounter at Bobby Short's apartment in 1977 (unusual, as Alberta rarely socialized during those years) introduced her to Charles Bourgeois, to whom she admitted "I've written a few songs, too." After two thrilling choruses of "**Down Hearted Blues**" Charles called Barney Josephson, which led to an invitation to perform at his popular Village club The Cookery. Word quickly spread and she became the toast of New York, every table packed with old and new fans.

In the award winning documentary *My Castle's Rockin'*, we get a chance to hear Alberta perform at the Cookery while examining her well-deserved place in music history. Alberta's voice at 82 was strong and sure, deepened and enriched by her years. Every gesture, coy eye movement, hand-on-hip stance spoke of a woman who knew how important the story of a song is to an audience, and how to bring out each lyric as if it were a gift. Her unexpected comeback – which led to sold out concert halls, and to the White House to sing for President Carter – lasted until Alberta Hunter was 89 years old, when age finally caught up with her. She died peacefully in her armchair.

SELECTED SONGLIST...

- CHIRPING THE BLUES
- CAN'T TELL THE DIFFERENCE AFTER DARK
- DOWN HEARTED BLUES
- AMTRAK BLUES
- HE'S GOT A PUNCH LIKE JOE LOUIS
- YOU GOT TO REAP WHAT YOU SOW
- THE LOVE I HAVE FOR YOU
- REMEMBER MY NAME
- TWO FISTED, DOUBLE JOINTED, ROUGH & READY MAN
- MY CASTLE'S ROCKIN'

SUGGESTED LISTENING...

Most of Alberta Hunter's earlier recordings don't show off her voice very well – due to poor recording equipment. But download her version of "**Down Hearted Blues**" as an essential part of your music library.

Songs We Taught Your Mother - Lucille Hegamin, Victoria Spivey, Alberta Hunter - (1961) a must have!

The Legendary Alberta Hunter: '34 London Sessions - (re-mastered in 1989) Alberta shows off a different aspect of her range singing popular songs with a Big Band, very good recording quality.

Alberta Hunter with Lovie Austin's Blues Serenaders - (Chicago – The Living Legends) 1961

Amtrak Blues - OBc Label, 1978

SOURCES...

Alberta Hunter: A Celebration in Blues, Frank C. Taylor with Gerald Cook, McGraw Hill Books, 1984.

Stormy Weather: The Music and Lives of a Century of Jazzwomen, Linda Dahl, Pantheon Books, 1984

Just For a Thrill: Lil Hardin Armstrong, First Lady of Jazz, James L. Dickerson, Cooper Square Press, 2002.

My Castle's Rockin', VIEW Video Jazz Series, 1992, DVD-don't miss this award winning documentary packed with live and rare footage of Ms Hunter.

Albertson, Chris. "Talking at the Cookery, part 1 and part 2." Retrieved August 2011, http://stomp-off.blogspot.com/2011/04/talking-at-cookery.

ALBERTA
HUNTER
DOWNHEARTED BLUES
LIVE AT THE COOKERY

Beautiful DREAMLAND
WM. BOTTOMS Prop. and Mgr. 3520 STATE STREET
Chicago's Finest Place of Amusement
REAL ENTERTAINERS   PERFECT DANCE FLOOR
OLLIE POWERS' "HARMONY SYNCOPATORS"
25 CENTS ADMISSION
EXCEPT ON SAT., SUN. AND HOLIDAYS
SPECIAL MATINEE ON THURSDAYS AT POPULAR PRICE
YOU WILL BE PROUD OF "DREAMLAND"

ALBERTA HUNTER
Complete Recorded Works In Chronological Order
VOLUME 4
1927–1946
Featuring:
FATS WALLER
CHARLIE SHAVERS
BUSTER BAILEY
LIL ARMSTRONG
EDDIE HEYWOOD
AND OTHERS
document RECORDS
DOCD-5425

Bessie Smith

London premiere of Showboat

DORIS FISHER
1915 – 2003
Queen of the Jukebox

Doris Fisher grew up in a home built upon Popular Song. Her father, Fred Fisher, practically ruled Tin Pan Alley in the 1920's, having written "**Chicago (That Toddlin' Town)**," "**Your Feet's Too Big**," "**I'd Rather Be Blue Over You**," "**Dardanella**," and "**Peg O' My Heart**." Doris and her brothers grew up tiptoeing around their New York house to avoid waking their father who had spent all night writing on one of his three pianos, often using his favorite – an upright installed in his bathroom. Sleep in the Fisher household might be interrupted when Fred would decide to invite all the performers from Connie's Inn in Harlem over for an after-hours party. The house was filled with people from every walk of life: singers, dancers, politicians, and jazz artists.

Small wonder that all the Fisher children tried their hand at songwriting. Her brother Dan wrote "**Good Morning Heartache**" and her brother Marvin wrote "**When Sunny Gets Blue**." But it was big sister Doris who came up with so many hit songs that jazz critic Leonard Feather dubbed her "The Queen of the Jukebox."

Doris liked to tell an anecdote in which she approached her father upon finishing college and said, "Well Pops, I'm done with school. Now what should I do with my life?" And he replied, in his thick German accent: "For you, two choices. One, get married. Two, become a songwriter." And so she became a songwriter.

She actually married four times while she was a songwriter, but why ruin a good story? In a New York Post article from 1936, Doris admitted that it wasn't easy being involved with a composer, as she "ate, drank, slept, dreamed songs...sometimes I've got to get up in the middle of the night to get a song out of my system."

In 1936, pretty, petite and barely 21, Doris landed a coveted spot as featured vocalist with Eddie Duchin's band on the Pall Mall Radio Show. Not wanting to get her breakthrough her father's name, she used the pseudonym "Penny Wise." In her spare time she created the musical score for Harry Richman's new Cotton Club revue. She led her own touring band for a while (Penny Wise and her Wise Guys), but a tune she had written, "**Tutti Frutti**" (no relation to the Little Richard song), was a big hit for Slim Gaillard, coaxing Doris into becoming a full time songwriter. A collaboration in 1940 with her father Fred on a song called "**Whispering Grass**," became a huge hit for the Ink Spots.

But it was a ride in the Brill Building elevator that introduced Doris to her favorite lyricist, Allan Roberts. In 1945 alone, a dizzyingly productive year, Fisher and Roberts dominated the popular music charts. They gave Louis Prima his break out hits "**Zooma Zooma**" and "**Angelina.**" Bing Crosby and the Andrew Sisters recorded "**Good Good Good,**" then there was "**Into Each Life Some Rain Must Fall**" (Ink Spots, Ella Fitzgerald), "**Invitation to the Blues**" (Ella Mae Morse, Anita Ellis), "**That Ole Devil Called Love**" (Billie Holliday, Billy Eckstine), "**You Always Hurt the One You Love**" (Mills Brothers, Spike Jones, Connie Francis). Doris Fisher's melodies often had a bluesy, drawling quality which no doubt was the reason Pearl Bailey approached this successful team to develop material for her. Fisher and Roberts not only wrote some great songs for Ms. Bailey, they also helped develop the spoken patter and definable character which made "**Tired**" and "**That's Good Enough For Me**" some of Pearl Bailey's most beloved repertoire.

Movie mogul Harry Cohn, impressed at this stream of hit songs, invited Fisher and Roberts to come to Hollywood in 1945.

On their first day of work, they were challenged to come up with a song for Rita Hayworth to sing in her new film "**Gilda.**" After a few hours, they came back with "**Put the Blame on Mame,**" followed by "**Amado Mio**" a few days later. These songs, although actually sung by Anita Ellis on screen, became synonymous with Rita Hayworth's sinuous, cheeky, explosive onscreen persona. Fisher and Roberts kept busy during their Hollywood years, contributing the music to *Down To Earth, The Lady From Shanghai, Singin' In The Corn, Strawberry Roan, Dead Reckoning, The Thrill Of Brazil*, and *The Corpse Came C.O.D.*

Doris liked to say that she "reinvented herself every few years." In 1949 she quit the music business and married Charles Gershenson, a Detroit real estate magnate. For many years she enjoyed raising her son and daughter, while being quite the sparkling social hostess. Always interested in design, she indulged this passion and

amassed an important collection of pre-Revolutionary War antiques. The marriage ended in the 1960's. Doris moved to Los Angeles, and opened two home design stores, while she continued her study of American antiques. Doris became such an authority on the subject that Jackie Kennedy asked for her help in finding key pieces during the 1961 restoration of the White House.

Doris Fisher never liked to brag about her accomplishments, and even her children seemed unaware of the important music catalogue their mother owned. During her last few years, a chance encounter brought Doris in touch with Harold Jacobs and Roy Bishop, two music lovers and sheet music collectors. When Harold became president of the National Sheet Music Society, he made it a point to honor Doris, sparking interest in her remarkable songwriting career and re-introducing her to new and old fans, which culminated

in some television appearances, including a tribute from ASCAP, for whom she penned so many hits.

Modern jazz and pop acts such as Alison Moyet, Dianne Reeves and Pink Martini continue to hit gold by recording Doris Fisher songs. Michael Feinstein remembered her fondly as "feisty, tenacious, talented" upon learning of her passing at the age of 87.

SOURCES...

From the Bowery to Broadway: Lew Fields and the Roots of American Popular Theater, Armond Fields & Marc Fields, Oxford University Press, 1993

red Fisher Biography, Retrieved June 2009, om Songwriter's Hall of Fame, http://www.ongwritershalloffame.org/exhibits/bio/C259

SCAP Songwriter Doris Fisher Dies at 87, Pauline ack, February 19, 2003. Retrieved June 2009, http://ww.ascap.com/press/2003/dorisfisher_012303.html

urs for a Song: The Women of Tin Pan Alley, erry Benes (Dir), PBS - American Masters, 1999, DVD.

oris Fisher, Mini Biography, Retrieved August 2009, ttp://www.imdb.com/name/nm0279463/bio

sher, Dan. *Daddy, You've Been a Mother To Me,* npublished memoir.

acobs, Harold, June 16, 2011. Personal interview ith P.Rose.

Doris Fisher", The Song Sheet, A Publication of the ational Sheet Music Society, January – February 2000.

ennis McClellan, "Doris Fisher, 87; Song Composer." anuary 17, 2003, Los Angeles Times

SELECTED SONGLIST...

- PUT THE BLAME ON MAME
- INVITATION TO THE BLUES
- WHISPERING GRASS
- INTO EACH LIFE SOME RAIN MUST FALL
- TUTTI FRUTTI
- THAT OLE DEVIL CALLED LOVE
- AMADO MIO
- ANGELINA (THE WAITRESS AT THE PIZZERIA)
- ZOOMA ZOOMA
- YOU ALWAYS HURT THE ONE YOU LOVE
- EITHER IT'S LOVE OR IT ISN'T
- FIFTEEN YEARS (AND I'M STILL DOING TIME)
- TAMPICO
- TIRED

SUGGESTED LISTENING...

"That Ole Devil Called Love" – Billie Holliday, Alison Moyet

"Amado Mio" – Anita Ellis, Pink Martini

"Tired" and "That's Good Enough For Me" – Pearl Bailey

"Tampico" – Stan Kenton and June Christy

"Invitation to the Blues" – Ella Mae Morse

"Angelina" – Louis Prima

"Into Each Life Some Rain Must Fall" – Ink Spots and Ella Fitzgerald

"You Always Hurt the One You Love" – Mills Brothers, but don't miss the Spike Jones version!

BILLIE HOLIDAY'S
THAT OLE DEVIL CALLED LOVE
Words and Music by DORIS FISHER and ALLAN ROBERTS

1.25
In U.S.A.

DORIS FISHER MUSIC CORP.
Sole Selling Agent
FISHER MUSIC CORP.
1619 Broadway, New York, N.Y. 10019

A smile in her eyes has PENNY WISE. Meet the new singing and band sensation of the White Way, who writes her songs as well as singing and directing them. Versatile? That's PENNY'S middle name.
(Photo, Murray Korman)

COLUMBIA PICTURES presents

Rita HAYWORTH
as
Gilda
with
Glenn FORD

GEORGE MACREADY · JOSEPH CALLE

SCREENPLAY BY MARION PARSONNET

Produced by   Directed by
VIRGINIA VAN UPP · CHARLES VIDOR

ris Fisher, 87; Co-Wrote String of 1940s
s Recorded by Bing Crosby, Many Others

IS McLELLAN
Writer

Fisher, who with lyri-
Roberts wrote "Put
e on Mame," "You Al-
rt the One You Love,"
ch Life Some Rain
ll," "Tampico" and a
other 1940s hits, has
e was 87.

r, whose songs were
by everyone from El-
rald and Bing Crosby
Autry and the Ink
ied Jan. 15 of causes

"kept yelling, 'Schmaltz it up,
kid. Schmaltz it up.'

"After it was finished, I
burst out crying and moaned,
'This is corn. You can have my
share for $5.' He gave me the
money. Then we sold it, and
before I knew what hit me, we
had made $25,000. Needless to
say, the $5 deal was called off,
and I got my share of the number back in a hurry."

After coming out to Hollywood in 1945 to write music
under contract to Columbia
Pictures, Fisher and Roberts

JEROME H. REMICK & COMPANY. MUSIC PUBLISHE

WHITNEY WARNER MUSIC

MUSIC PUBLISHERS.

JEROME H. REMICK & COMPANY

Tin Pan Alley

TUTTI FRUTTI

SUGAR BOWL

Introduced & featured by
"SLIM AND SLAM"
WRITERS OF "FLAT FOOT FLOOGEE"

written by
DORIS FISHER
and
"SLIM" GAILLARD

YOU ALWAYS HURT THE ONE YOU LOVE

Words and Music by ALLAN ROBERTS and DORIS FISHER

SUNG BY
THE MILLS BROTHERS

DOROTHY FIELDS
1905 – 1974
One of the Guys

"It's hard slave labor. Ask anyone who writes... it's slave labor and I love it." Dorothy Fields, **An Evening with Dorothy Fields**

Dorothy Fields had a style of lyric writing that was breezy, colloquial, as easily spoken as sung, and easy on a singer's tongue. Using everyday details of life, she could describe lofty emotions in a down-to-earth way that never betrayed how many hours she labored to make it sound effortless. Sammy Cahn and Stephen Sondheim have both admiringly referred to various lyrics written by Dorothy Fields as 'perfect.'

When I mention the name "Dorothy Fields" on stage, I often get a blank look from the audience, or polite, thin applause. Then I list a few of her more than 400 titles: "**I Can't Give You Anything But Love**," "**On the Sunny Side of the Street**," "**Don't Blame Me**," "**The Way You Look Tonight**," "**Hey Big Spender**," and I'm met by a thunderous, happy wave of recognition.

Dorothy Fields was born in 1905 into the New York home of the well-known comic actor and producer, Lew Fields. Although her mother hoped to elevate her children beyond a life in show business, three out of four of her children ended up in the theater. Her brother Herb, in particular, was a gifted wordsmith and librettist and was constantly recruiting talented friends (Richard Rodgers, Lorenz Hart) to join him in creating a song, a show, a revue. This world of young song-crafters proved irresistible to a shy but lyrically clever girl like Dorothy. She would pitch an idea for a lyric or line so often that she was considered one of the guys, a role she enjoyed all of her life.

Richard Rodgers introduced Dorothy to fellow writer J. Fred Coots, and together they caught the attention of publisher Jack Mills. At Mills she teamed with Jimmy McHugh, who asked her to try her hand at writing lyrics for a revue at the Cotton Club. When Dorothy informed her father Lew of this endeavor, he was furious and argued: "Ladies don't write lyrics!" Dorothy quickly responded with a variation of one of Lew Fields' most famous lines: "I'm not a lady, I'm your daughter."

One of McHugh and Fields' early attempts was a song called "**I Can't Give You Anything But Love**." This tune "premiered" on three different occasions, yanked twice by producers after reviews called it "puerile, sickly" and "lousy." When the song finally caught on, it sold more than three million units of sheet music.

Her partnership with McHugh continued to strike big with "**On the Sunny Side of the Street**," "**Don't Blame Me**," and "**I'm in the Mood for Love**."

After moving to Hollywood to write for the major studios, Dorothy was paired with Jerome Kern, beginning a working friendship marked by great mutual respect and admiration (unusual for the brilliant, yet demanding, Kern). The pinnacle of their partnership was perhaps marked by the Astaire/Rogers movie *Swing Time*. For that one film alone, Fields and Kern wrote "**Pick Yourself Up**," "**A Fine Romance**," and "**The Way You Look Tonight**," which won them both an Oscar.

Recalling the creation of "**The Way You Look Tonight**," Dorothy Fields wrote:

> *The first time Jerry played that melody for me I had to leave the room because I started to cry. The release absolutely killed me. I couldn't stop, it was so beautiful.*
> <u>They're Playing Our Song</u>, by Max Wilk

Dorothy responded by giving us a lyric perfectly wed to the melody: touching, lilting and timeless.

Missing the vibrancy of Broadway, Dorothy moved back to New York in 1938. She married Eli Lahm, a New York clothing manufacturer. It was actually Stephen Sondheim's father Herbert (also in the clothing business) who introduced the pair – saying he "made a shiddach." Over the next few years Dorothy enjoyed teaming up with her brother Herb to write books and librettos, while raising her children David and Eliza.

Chief among these writing efforts are three Cole Porter vehicles, two starring Ethel Merman (*Something for the Boys* and *Mexican Hayride*).

Loving the play writer role and the thrill of Broadway production, she seized upon the idea to write a vehicle for Ms. Merman as gun-toting Annie Oakley – Jerome Kern was supposed to write the music and re-unite Dorothy with her favorite composer, but sadly, Kern died just before work began. Irving Berlin ably jumped to the task, with Dorothy and Herb Fields co-writing the book *Annie Get Your Gun*. Since Mr. Berlin always wrote his own lyrics, Dorothy Fields' graceful exit as co-songwriter exemplified her great qualities as team player, and the result

otthy and Herb Fields at work.

was a fantastic story, script and songbook which has been revived many times over.

These rich and productive years were halted in 1958 when the shocking death of her producer and close friend Mike Todd was tragically followed two days later by the sudden death of her brother Herb. And in a cruel progression, her beloved husband Eli died of a cerebral hemorrhage a few months later.

It was pianist and composer Cy Coleman who finally coaxed Dorothy Fields back to work in the late 60's with the musical *Sweet Charity*. The collaboration added two more remarkable feathers in her songwriting cap "**If My Friends Could See Me Now,**" and "**Hey Big Spender.**" Dorothy and Coleman continued their partnership a few years later with the excellent *Seesaw*. Although 25 years older than her colleagues, Dorothy Fields never lost the knack for finding the right 'voice' for each song, bringing in a modern vernacular that was never forced, and always matching the lyric to the character perfectly.

ASCAP president Stanley Adams said that "the Dorothy Fields catalogue was the most important and significant of any woman writer.".. not just by virtue

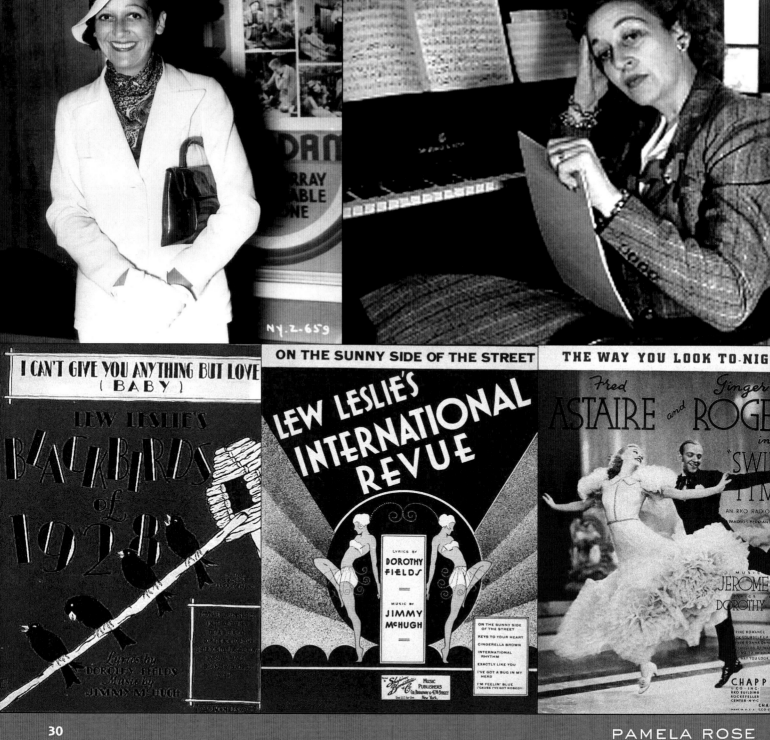

of the size and the scope of her catalogue but by the fact that over the years her songs have remained unflaggingly popular. One might argue that this statement would stand true even without the qualifier "woman writer." Her career, spanning 50 years, produced unforgettable hits in every decade and every medium available to her.

When interviewed by Henry Kane for his book **How To Write A Song**, she was asked why there weren't more women songwriters. Her reply was "I do *not* think that men have more talent," but noted that women often have to tend a home and raise a family, so that they simply don't have the time it takes to give it "the push needed, the going out and mixing" all so important in the basically self-employed career of music. One must always be looking for the next show, song, or collaborator.

And yet Dorothy did love family life, and with the steadfast support of her husband Eli, raised her two children, Eliza and David Lahm, while maintaining her career. David Lahm grew up to be a jazz pianist, recording artist and beloved fixture of the New York cabaret scene along with his vocalist wife Judy Kreston. When asked if he felt it was unusual to have such a hard working mother in show business, he replied that his mother didn't seem that different from the other mothers in their New York circles, with nannies and a busy social schedule. It was only later that he realized how charmed their particular circle was, with Hammersteins, Kerns, Sondheims and Rogers all about. He fondly recalled that she also had the maternal wisdom to unconditionally support David's early jazz career, although the strange sounds of Coltrane and Herbie Hancock certainly didn't appeal to her.

Dorothy Fields was remembered as impeccably dressed and groomed, while chain smoking and occasionally knocking down a few from her flask. Perhaps growing up surrounded by inventive, talented men made her figure out how to navigate the "boys' club" while having her own life. Wife, mother, sister, playwright, librettist and unforgettable lyricist, she not only married her talent to her personal life, she made it "a fine romance."

Jerome Kern, Dorothy Fields, George Gershwin

SOURCES...

From the Bowery to Broadway: Lew Fields and the Roots of American Popular Theater, Armond Fields & L. Marc Fields, Oxford University Press, 1993

Pick Youself Up: Dorothy Fields and the American Musical, Charlotte Greenspan, Oxford University Press, 2010

On the Sunny Side of the Street: The Life and Lyrics of Dorothy Fields, Deborah Grace Winer, Schirmer Books, 1997

They're Playing Our Song: Conversations with America's Classic Songwriters, Max Wilk, Delacorte Publishing, 1973

The Jews on Tin Pan Alley, Kenneth Aaron Kanter, Ktav Publishing House, 1982.

www.dorothyfields.co.uk – A superb website, painstakingly researched

An Evening with Dorothy Fields (CD) DRG label, 1972. A must listen experience for Dorothy Fields fans. Ms. Fields holds forth for an hour, telling us about her life, and how certain songs came to be, aided by a small Broadway cast.

SELECTED SONGLIST...

- ON THE SUNNY SIDE OF THE STREET
- I CAN'T GIVE YOU ANYTHING BUT LOVE
- DON'T BLAME ME
- BOJANGLES OF HARLEM
- I'M IN THE MOOD FOR LOVE
- MAKE THE MAN LOVE ME
- THE WAY YOU LOOK TONIGHT
- A FINE ROMANCE
- PICK YOURSELF UP (DUST YOURSELF OFF)
- HEY BIG SPENDER
- IF MY FRIENDS COULD SEE ME NOW

SUGGESTED LISTENING...

"'A Fine Romance'" – Ella Fitzgerald and Louis Armstrong

"The Way You Look Tonight" - Frank Sinatra (Nelson Riddle Arrangement) (But don't miss Fred Astaire's original recording, with his all so human, beseeching voice.)

"I Won't Dance"- Blossom Dearie, Verve Jazz Masters Series

"Make the Man Love Me"- Dinah Washington, Dinah Washington for Lovers

Dorothy Fields and Jimmy McHugh

PEGGY LEE
1920 – 2002
Singer-Songwriter

Peggy Lee had a voice that caressed each note, and the word 'sultry' is used in every article written about her. She approached rhythm in a relaxed, confident way that we learned in later years to term 'soulful.' Like Frank Sinatra and Louis Armstrong, her accomplishments as a musician were almost eclipsed by her famous persona.

Yet few people are aware of how prolific a songwriter Peggy Lee was. Writing at first with her guitarist husband Dave Barbour, she later worked with collaborators as diverse as Harold Arlen, Duke Ellington, Quincy Jones, Marian McPartland and Michel Legrand. Peggy produced hit after hit for vinyl, television, Broadway, Hollywood, and even animated features.

Born Norma Egstrom in North Dakota, she lost her mother at age four, then suffered at the hands of a physically abusive step-mother. She recalled listening intently to the radio broadcasts coming in from Kansas City, particularly loving the Blues singers and the rhythm-driven Count Basie Band. Breaking first into radio at age fourteen, she ran away to join a string of regional bands, until she was finally spotted by Benny Goodman to replace Helen Forrest in his big band. In 1943 her version of "**Why Don't You Do Right?**" made her one of the most popular young singers in the U.S.

But a budding romance with Benny Goodman's guitarist Dave Barbour caused the bandleader to enforce his strict rule about no band romances, and Peggy made the decision to retire and marry Barbour. One year later she signed with Capitol as a solo artist and started collaborating with her husband, writing a string of songs that hit big. "**What More Can a Woman Do?**" (1945) was picked up and recorded by a young Sarah Vaughn, and was also an R & B single for Big Maybelle Merriweather.

In 1946, Peggy's song "**I Don't Know Enough About You**" became a major hit for Capitol, and "**It's a Good Day**" was used as one of the opening numbers in the Susan Hayward film, *With a Song in My Heart*. In 1948 she wrote "**Mañana**," which topped the charts for nine weeks. On every one of her dozens of albums, Peggy made sure to include a few original songs, anticipating the classification of singer-songwriter by at least 20 years.

In 1958, her version of Little Willie John's "**Fever**" became her most famous recording, with her two original verses breathing fresh life into the song. ('Romeo

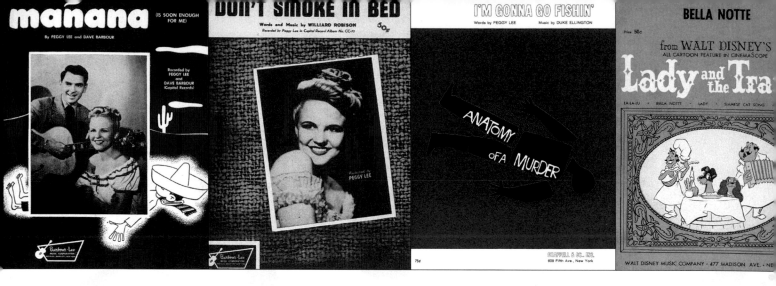

& Juliet', 'Captain Smith & Pocahontas').

Peggy often started with a melody and lyric in mind, and then sought out a writing partner to help her finish the song. In this way she co-wrote "**I Love Being Here With You**" (with Bill Schluger), a venerable workhorse of a song that is in every jazz singer's repertoire, the haunting, bittersweet "**Don't Smoke in Bed**" (with Willard Robison – Peggy took her name off the publishing credits to give the struggling Robison a financial boost.)

Peggy also could make a song come alive with her singer's knowledge of what made a good lyric and a great phrase. In this way she contributed lyrics to "**Johnny Guitar**" (Victor Young), "**Then Was Then**" (with Cy Coleman), and of course, "**Bella Notte**," "**Siamese Cat Song**" and "**He's a Tramp**" (with Sonny Burke for Walt Disney).

She was paid $1,000 by Walt Disney to compose six songs (with collaborator Sonny Burke) for the animated feature *Lady and the Tramp*. At the bargain rate of $3,500, she was the voice of four of the characters and sang in the film as well (Peggy played the role of "Darling," "Peg," who sang "**He's a Tramp**" and also the singing Siamese cats.) Disney had brokered hundreds of these unfair deals with artists, and successfully fought off many later royalty claims. Their unofficial tagline in the industry was "Don't Mess with the Mouse." But when the film was released in video in the 1970's, the estimated additional $90 million in sales to Disney was too much for the determined Ms. Lee to leave alone, and after a fifteen year court battle, she successfully sued them for a landmark $3.8 million in back royalties. She was seventy by the time the settlement came through, and

perfectly comfortable without it, but that wasn't the point. The settlement liberated musicians and artists from Disney's draconian policies.

She was a famous perfectionist about her work, with an intense work ethic she said she learned from Benny Goodman. Peggy was adored by a wide spectrum of music lovers: jazz fans who loved every hip release off her LP **Mink Jazz** and pop fans who adored her version of Lieber and Stoller's "**Is That All There Is?**" A twelve-time Grammy nominated artist (who lost out almost every time to Ella Fitzgerald), she received a Lifetime Achievement Award in 1995. In 1955, she was nominated for an Academy Award for her role in *Pete Kelly's Blues*, playing a hard drinking, world-weary singer.

But it was Peggy Lee's unflagging passion for songwriting, no matter the vehicle, that amassed her surprisingly large portfolio of music. With Duke Ellington she wrote "**I'm Gonna Go Fishin'**" for the movie *Anatomy of a Murder*. Then in 1961, with Harold Arlen, she wrote "**Happy with the Blues**" for a television special on Arlen's music. (**Happy with the Blues** became the title of Arlen's biography.) She later co-wrote songs for the Jane Fonda movie *Joy House* (1964), the Carl Reiner movie *The Russians Are Coming! The Russians Are Coming!* (1966), the Cary Grant movies *Walk, Don't Run* (1966), the Alan Arkin movie *The Heart Is a Lonely Hunter* (1968), the Charles Bronson movie *Rider on the Rain* (1971), and *The Nickel Ride* (1974).

In 1983, she composed 22 originals in preparation for a Broadway show about her life, called *Peg*. Sadly, illness prevented her from ever performing this work.

Sexy, sultry Peggy Lee — generations of singer-songwriters owe you so much for paving the way.

Peggy and Dave Barbour

SELECTED SONGLIST...

- IT'S A GOOD DAY
- MANANA
- I LOVE BEING HERE WITH YOU
- I DON'T KNOW ENOUGH ABOUT YOU
- DON'T SMOKE IN BED
- I'M GONNA GO FISHIN'
- HAPPY WITH THE BLUES
- WHAT MORE CAN A WOMAN DO?
- LADY AND THE TRAMP:
    SIAMESE CAT SONG
    BELLA NOTTE
    HE'S A TRAMP

SUGGESTED LISTENING...

Most of Miss Peggy Lee's songs have been rendered perfectly by the writer herself. For a list of her compositions and which LP's host original songs, go to www.peggylee.com

However, a few other notable mentions:

"Don't Smoke in Bed" — Nina Simone, Julie London, k.d.lang.

"I Love Being Here With You" — Ernestine Anderson, Diana Krall

"It's a Good Day" — Mavis Rivers, Judy Garland

"The Shining Sea" — Tony Bennett

‌OURCES...

‌ever: The Life and Music of Miss Peggy Lee, ‌eter Richmond, Henry Holt and Company, 2006

‌tormy Weather: The Music and Lives of a Century ‌f Jazzwomen, Linda Dahl, Pantheon Books, 1984

‌iss Peggy Lee: An Autobiography, Peggy Lee, ‌loomsbury Press (UK) 2002

‌ww.peggylee.com (A superb website, filled with ‌n enormous discography, photos and articles)

‌Miss Peggy Lee, (1999). Retrieved June 1, 2009, from ‌ttp://www.songwritershalloffame.org/index.php. ‌xhibits/bio/C166

BERNICE PETKERE
1901 - 2000
Queen of Tin Pan Alley

"*I never was pals with the other women composers, or even the male ones. You had to be business-like about music, and I was. Only a couple of music executives ever got what I called 'fresh' with me, and I let them have it, smack in the face like you never saw.*"

This scrappy, down-to-earth attitude surely characterizes composer and lyricist Bernice Petkere (pronounced Pet-Care). She began her show business career at the tender age of five, on the Pantages Vaudeville Circuit. Paired up with an aunt, Bernice held up her end of a duo called "Baby Dolls." The early push to the stage seemed to suit her very well, as she stayed in show business much of her life.

Bernice studied voice at the Henshaw Conservatory of Music in Chicago, and then taught herself to play piano as a teenager. Self taught or not, she was good enough to secure work as a pianist in the prestigious music publishing firm of Waterson, Berlin and Snyder in New York, while doing some singing in various dance bands.

Although Bernice started writing songs when she was 19 years old, it wasn't until eleven years later in 1931, that she published her first song, "**Starlight (Help Me Find the One I Love)**." Sitting in a Manhattan bar, she scribbled notes to the music on the back of a menu, and teamed up with Joe Young to finish the lyric idea. Published by Irving Berlin, the song was recorded by Bing Crosby during his breakout year of 1931, on the Brunswick Label. While not as well remembered as some of his later Decca sides, "**Starlight**" did establish his relaxed, crooning style and a whistling solo that was often his trademark.

Irving Berlin was so impressed by her work that he asked her to be a staff writer for his publishing company. Over the next few years she wrote many popular songs, including both music and lyrics to "**Close Your Eyes**" and the lovely "**By a Rippling Stream**." With lyricists Joe Young and Ned Washington she penned "**Did You Mean What You Said Last Night?**," "**The Lady I Love**," and "**Stay Out of My Dreams**." She once received a letter delivered by the Post Office to her New York apartment with no other address than "*Bernice Petkere, Queen of Tin Pan Alley*."

After marrying Fred Berrens (music director at CBS), she worked steadily composing theme music for many radio shows. With Joe Young, Bernice composed "**Lullaby of the Leaves**" for the 1932 Broadway revue *Chamberlain Brown's Scrap Book*. Although the show didn't last more than a dozen

performances, the tune was introduced on the radio by Freddie Berrens and his Orchestra, leading to sides recorded by Ben Selvin and Connee Boswell. This intriguing composition has become a genuine jazz standard. Compositionally rich, with a wistful, slightly mournful melody, it was a favorite vehicle for Art Tatum, Dizzy Gillespie and continues to be played by jazz artists all around the globe.

Moving to Los Angeles in the late 30's gave Ms. Petkere the opportunity to write film scores, and her song "**It's All So New to Me**" was performed by Joan Crawford in *Ice Follies*. Later Bernice also collaborated on story and screenplay for the film *Sabotage Squad*.

The frank and unvarnished persona of Bernice Petkere was perhaps best revealed in her Los Angeles Times obituary. When her apartment was converted into a condo out of her price range, a fan and investor bought the unit, stipulating she be allowed to stay there as long as she lived. Upon thanking her benefactor, Ms. Petkere is said to have added: "I hope you won't be offended if I live a long time." She died at the age of 98.

SELECTED SONGLIST...

- STARLIGHT (HELP ME FIND THE ONE I LOVE)
- CLOSE YOUR EYES
- LULLABY OF THE LEAVES
- BY A RIPPLING STREAM
- DID YOU MEAN WHAT YOU SAID LAST NIGHT?
- STAY OUT OF MY DREAMS
- HAPPY LITTLE FARMER
- A MILE A MINUTE
- THE LADY I LOVE
- IT'S ALL SO NEW TO ME

SUGGESTED LISTENING...

"Lullaby of the Leaves" – Art Tatum, Connee Boswell (1932, lovely vocal), Chet Atkins (Hi-Fi in Focus), The Ventures 1961 (surf guitar meets jazz.)

"Close Your Eyes" – Kurt Elling (1995 Blue Note), Ella Fitzgerald, Queen Latifah (as Dana Owens)

SOURCES...

The Unsung Songwriters, Warren W. Vache, Rowman and Littlefield Publishers, Inc., 2000

The American Popular Ballad of the Golden Era, 1924-1950, Allen Forte, Princeton University Press, 1995

Peter Mintun, 2009, *Bernice Petkere*, Retrieved January 2010, from http://www.imdb.com/name/nm0677675/bio

Los Angeles Times, Obituary, January 12, 2000

Yours for a Song: The Women of Tin Pan Alley, Terry Benes (Dir), PBS - American Masters, 1999, DVD.

KAY SWIFT

1897–1993

Keeper of the Flame

*K*ay Swift's life reads like a New York Jazz Age fairytale: "*There was once a lovely young classical composer who fell in love with two men. One was from Wall Street, one from Tin Pan Alley....*"

And yet her full story is much like her music: nuanced, surprising, beautiful, wistful.

Katharine Faulkner Swift was born in New York City in 1897. Her father Samuel was a highly regarded music critic. Although the family often struggled financially, they always found a way to develop their daughter's evident passion for music. At age six she loved Wagnerian opera, and began composing her own pieces on piano. By the time Katharine was eight, Samuel's contacts with the classical world enabled her to study at the Institute of Musical Art in New York (later known as Julliard, co-founded by her future husband's family), putting her in the hands of superb and exacting teachers. Young Katharine thrived under the rigorous tutelage, excelling at orchestration, advanced composition and theory.

Her father's sudden death in 1914 ended her dreams of becoming a classical composer, and Katharine entered the working world as a rehearsal pianist. While accompanying a chamber trio, she met James Paul Warburg, the dashing son of a well-known American Jewish-German banking family. His father Paul (who helped found the Federal Reserve), was delighted with the match, as he admired Katharine's work ethic, earnest ambition and ability.

If Katharine was intimidated by this leap from genteel, shabby poverty into a dazzling life of luxury with a staff of servants and a whirlwind social life, she never let it show. The union seemed to invigorate both of them: James proved himself to be just as adept and brilliant a financial mind as his father and grandfather, and in between the birth of their three daughters Katharine resumed her serious studies of music, writing a fugue a week, and performing in small concerts.

The life of the Warburgs in those heady, pre-Depression days seems like scenes from an F. Scott Fitzgerald novel. New York in 1920 was bursting with energy – skirts were getting shorter, rhythms were becoming more syncopated, it was the Jazz Age in all its glory. Parties at the home of Katharine and James in their chic East 70's townhouse boasted a guest list that often included Dorothy Parker, Robert Benchley, Lorenz Hart, Richard Rodgers and F. Scott himself.

George Gershwin appeared at one these parties in 1925. This brash, charismatic Tin Pan Alley songwriter had just presented his cross-over masterpiece, "**Rhapsody in Blue**," at Carnegie Hall and was bursting with ideas and confidence. The son of Russian-Jewish immigrants, George's limited musical education never dampened his ideas, big music concepts or huge ego.

They were truly each other's musical, and then romantic, soul mates. Gershwin introduced Katharine to a new musical world of Jazz and Broadway, which up until then she had found repetitive and limited. And she in turn, shared her sophisticated sense of composition and scoring. She would take quick dictation as he composed, providing suggestions for counterpoint and orchestration. Many of his manuscripts are written partly in his hand, partly in hers. They shared musical notebooks, jotting down themes and melodies, he starting at one end of the pad, she from the other. He dubbed her 'Kay' – and this was the name she preferred from that day forward, Kay Swift.

By becoming a rehearsal pianist for Rodgers and Hart's *A Connecticut Yankee*, Kay absorbed everything she could about Broadway and popular music. Her banker husband James, who had always enjoyed writing light verse, started writing lyrics for Kay under the pseudonym Paul James.

After an initial period of rejection, Kay and 'Paul' began to place songs in Broadway revues from 1928 through 1930. Their haunting song "**Can't We Be Friends**" was debuted by the scandalous Libby Holman in *The Little Show*.

In 1930, with the Warburg marriage strained and the stock market crashing, the Swift/James team undertook the remarkable gamble of mounting their own musical, *Fine and Dandy*, with a book by Donald Ogden Stewart. The unforgettable songs "**Can This Be Love**" and of course "**Fine and Dandy**," outlasted the run of the successful show and earned Kay Swift her place in the Great American Songbook.

For the next few years, as James Warburg toiled within President Roosevelt's administration to restore the banking industry, Kay worked behind the scenes with George Gershwin as his increasingly indispensable musical confidante and romantic partner. There seems little doubt that these remarkably productive years in his life (1930 – 1934) in which he produced five Broadway shows, scored films, composed classical concert works and mounted his masterpiece *Porgy and Bess*, were made possible through Kay's assistance.

In 1934, Kay Swift was commissioned by the American Ballet of New York to compose a piece for its opening performance, *Alma Mater*, featuring a newly arrived George Balanchine. Yet this achievement was dampened by the dissolution of Kay's marriage to James Warburg.

Now a single woman at the height of the Depression, Kay secured work as staff composer for Radio City Music Hall, writing a new song a week for the Rockettes.

When the Gershwin brothers left for Hollywood in 1936, Kay and George agreed to break all contact for a year in order to re-assess the potential for their future. It is said that he called her shortly before he was to return to New York, saying "I'm coming back for the two of us."

George Gershwin's sudden death in 1937 from a brain tumor was a tragedy experienced publicly in the music world, but quite privately for Kay Swift. She instructed his brother Ira to destroy all of her letters to George, and did the same, leaving only the stories she later told her children and grandchildren.

Kay and George Gershwin

While serving as Director of Music for the 1939 New York World's Fair, Kay met rancher Faye Hubbard and moved to Oregon. Her fictional account of that marriage, *Who Could Ask for Anything More?* was turned into the 1950 film *Never a Dull Moment* featuring three of Kay's songs.

In 1952 Kay was back on Broadway,

having collaborated on a one woman show featuring Cornelia Otis Skinner called *Paris '90*, a delightful series of vignettes set in the Paris of Toulouse-Lautrec's day. When Samuel Goldwyn Pictures filmed *Porgy and Bess* they hired Kay to tour and lecture upon Gershwin's masterpiece. Alfred Stern commissioned her throughout the years to produce music for World Fairs and Expos.

In 1993 Kay Swift passed away in New York. She was 96. Her lifelong efforts to promote and celebrate George's music has been generously acknowledged by the Gershwin Trust. Her granddaughter, author Katharine Weber, maintains the Kay Swift Memorial Trust dedicated to preserving and promoting the music of Kay Swift.

Kay and husband James Warburg

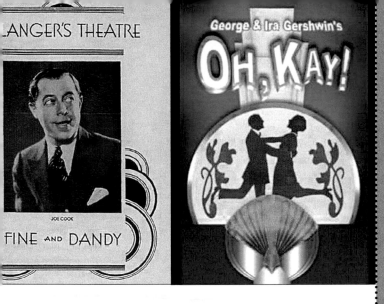

George & Ira Gershwin's

OH, KAY!

JOE COOK

FINE AND DANDY

SELECTED SONGLIST...

- CAN THIS BE LOVE
- FINE AND DANDY
- CAN'T WE BE FRIENDS?
- WHISTLING IN THE DARK
- ALMA MATER (BALANCHINE BALLET)
- I'LL HIT A NEW HIGH
- LET'S GO EAT WORMS IN THE GARDEN
- NOBODY BREAKS MY HEART
- ONCE YOU FIND YOUR GUY
- SAWING A WOMAN IN HALF
- STARTING AT THE BOTTOM
- UP AMONG THE CHIMNEY POTS

SUGGESTED LISTENING...

"Can't We Be Friends?"

Frank Sinatra, **In the Wee Small Hours**

Ella Fitzgerald and Louis Armstrong,
Ella & Louis, Polygram Records

"Can This Be Love"

Bobby Short, **How's Your Romance?**
Tellarc Records

"Fine and Dandy"

Barbra Streisand, **People**

Django Reinhardt, **Jazz in Paris, vol 9**

Art Tatum, **Fine and Dandy**

SOURCES...

Fine and Dandy: The Life and Work of Kay Swift, Vicki Ohl, Yale University Press 2004.

The Memory of All That, Katharine Weber, Crown Publishers, 2011.

The American Popular Ballad of the Golden Era 1924-1950, Allen Forte, Princeton University Press, 1995

Yours for a Song: The Women of Tin Pan Alley, Terry Benes (Dir), PBS - American Masters, 1999, DVD.

New York Times, Obituary, Friday January 29, 1993

Kay Swift Website: http://www.kayswift.com

MARIA GREVER
1894 – 1951
The Heart of Mexico

Although her name is rarely recognized these days in the United States, this busy songwriter published more than 850 songs in her lifetime, many of which are still well known in Mexico, Spain and much of Latin America. Mention 'Maria Grever' in these countries, and it's as if you've brought up the name 'Irving Berlin.'

Popular legend has it that Maria Grever was born onboard the ship that carried her mother from her native Mexico to join her husband in Spain. It's only a romantic tale – but befitting for the woman who united European and homegrown North American music in her work. Maria Grever spent her musical career moving between continental orchestration, light opera and the folk melodies she loved and learned at her mother's knee.

Maria Joaquina de la Portilla Torres was actually born in Mexico in 1894, and grew up in wealth and comfort, traveling frequently between Spain and Mexico. She started composing songs at age six, and as a youth studied with Claude Debussy and Franz Lenhard in France. She was passionate about music, about opera, about singing, about love, about life. At age 18 Maria published her first song "**A Una Ola**" ("**To a Wave**") which sold 3 million copies of sheet music.

At the age of twenty-two, Maria met and married Leon A. Grever, an American oil company executive, who was best man in her sister's wedding. It was love at first sight, and they were married four days after they met. Leon Grever brought Maria to New York, and it was there that Maria's international career was launched. Maria's music was heard live in many of New York City's concert halls, and she also toured in Latin America and Europe.

She staged many concerts featuring her soprano voice and original music, but she was also happy to share the spotlight with those whom she mentored, such as Agustín Lara, the beloved Mexican poet-composer. She delighted in celebrating her Mexican culture through music. It was her "desire and ambition…to present native melodies and rhythms authentically, but with the flexibility necessary to call to the universal ear."

In 1920, Grever was contracted by Paramount Studios and 20th century Fox to score the soundtracks to several of its Hispanice-American themed movies. MGM featured her songs in the Esther Williams classic, *Bathing Beauty*.

Maria's romantic songs popularized the bolero tradition of Latin America. "**Júrame**" was often performed by Enrico Caruso, and more recently, Placido Domingo and Andrea Bocelli. She seemed to be an endless fount of material for films, dance programs, Broadway and revues. "**Volveré**," "**Así**," "**Yo No Se**," "**Magic is the Moonlight**," "**Lamento Gitano**," "**My First, My Last, My Only**" all enjoyed great popularity with Big Bands of the era, as did a lighthearted song called "**Ti-Pi-Tin**" which was a hit for the Andrews Sisters in an English version. The original Spanish version is considered a timeless classic.

In 1934 Maria she wrote a bolero called "**Cuando Vuelva a tu Lado**" with a gorgeous, unforgettable melody that Benny Goodman recorded. Later the Dorsey Brothers (with Bob Crosby on vocals) recorded a new version of the song with an English lyric and title provided by lyricist Stanley Adams, with whom Maria often collaborated. "**What a Diff'rence a Day Made**" was a hit in the 30's, but it was Dinah Washington's rendition of this song in 1958 that gave Maria Grever her most memorable, if posthumous, hit. Dinah won a Grammy that year for her recording, and this version was inducted into the Grammy Hall of Fame in 1998.

Just as there is a dramatic tale spun around her birth, legend has it that in 1948, Maria was so overcome upon hearing her friend and fellow singer Nestor Chayres interpret her song "**Vida Mia**" at Carnegie Hall, she suffered a paralyzing stroke. In 1949, she was awarded the prestigious Medalla del Corazon de Mexico (Medal of the Heart of Mexico). She was also named "Woman of the Americas" at a New York ceremony in honor of her fundraising efforts for the education of the Blind in Latin America. Maria Grever passed away in New York at the age of 57 on December 15, 1951. She was buried in Mexico.

The musical history of the Grever family did not stop with Maria's death. Grever's son Charles opened his own record label, Golden Sands Music Publishing, with

a branch in San Antonio, Texas, called Cara Records. Under the leadership of Maria's grandson Robert Grever, Cara Records became the "Motown of Tejano Music," recording every significant Tejano and Tejana act, including Selena.

Performer, mentor, teacher, humanitarian, Maria Grever was an inspiration indeed, but her strongest legacy is in her over 850 songs – published in many languages and countries. Quoting Bill Zeitung's liner notes from **Songs of Maria Grever**, "*[Her music] is on every hand, yet the name is only familiar to a few.*"

SOURCES...

Notable Hispanic American Women,
Diane Telgen, Jim Kamp, 1993

A History of Popular Music in America,
Sigmund Spaeth, Random House, 1962.

Zeitung, Bill (1956), **Songs of Maria Grever**,
(LP liner notes), RCA Records

Burr, Ramiro, "Maria Grever Biography."
Retrieved May 2011, from http://www.jrank.org/cultures/pages/3931/Mar%C3%ADa-Grever.html

SELECTED SONGLIST...

- A UNA OLA (TO A WAVE)
- CUANDO VUELVA A TU LADO (WHAT A DIFF'RENCE A DAY MADE)
- TI PI TIN
- JÚRAME
- VOLVERÉ
- LAMENTO GITANO
- MAGIC IS THE MOONLIGHT
- ESO ES MENTIRA
- ASÍ
- LERO, LERO FROM BRAZIL
- CANCIONERA
- THANKS FOR THE KISS
- BÉSAME

SUGGESTED LISTENING...

"**Júrame**"– Andrea Bocelli, Placido Domingo.

Cuando Me Vaya (When I leave). Dir: Tito Davison, 1954, available in DVD. Starring Libertad Lamarque. (In Spanish).

"**Ti-pi-tin**" – Andrews Sisters. But dont overlook Tony Randall singing this with the Muppets! Hugo Avendano has a lovely version as well.

Libertad Lamarque Canta Canciones de Maria Grever, 1956, RCA LP, (with a superb "Ti-pi-tin")

"**What a Diff'rence a Day Made**" – Dinah Washington, Aretha Franklin

TOT SEYMOUR
1889 – 1966

VEE LAWNHURST
1905 – 1992

Girl Songwriters

When lyricist Tot Seymour paired up with pianist/composer Vee Lawnhurst, they were so often at the top of the Hit Parade, that their publishing company, Famous Music, took out ads in the trade papers proudly calling them *"The first successful team of girl song writers in popular musical history!"* Collectively and together Tot Seymour and Vee Lawnhurst were pioneers in the new medium of radio. Their songs, though perhaps not well known today, were ubiquitous within the popular music landscape of the 1930's.

Born Grace Mann in New York City in 1889, Tot Seymour was already in demand as a lyric writer in the 1920's. A staff lyricist at Irving Berlin's publishing company, Waterson, Berlin and Snyder, she was one of the first women on Tin Pan Alley, and wrote special material for headliners Fannie Brice, Sophie Tucker and Mae West, as well as contributing to many of the Ziegfeld Follies. Soon she was collaborating with tunesmiths Sigmund Romberg and J. Fred Coots (with whom she wrote "**I Miss a Little Miss**"). Other hits included "**Swingin' on a Hammock**" and "**I'm Makin' Hay in the Moonlight (In My Baby's Arms)**."

Vee Lawnhurst (born Laura Lowenherz of New York City in 1905), had been busy wowing audiences with her superb piano playing. Vee's intricate, inventive playing style, preserved on many piano rolls, was so extraordinary that listeners swore that she must have been an invention; a pretend "Vee" who was really a number of skilled pianists edited together. But those who were lucky enough to hear her broadcast live every week as part of "Roxy's Gang" in the early 1920's live from the Capitol Theatre (a feat that made her one of radio's pioneer pianists) recognized her astonishing talent. Later she paired up with the very fine pianist Muriel Pollack and cut a number of records featuring the duo. "We worked well together," reminisced Vee in an interview with Peter Mintun. "I couldn't read much, and she couldn't improvise, so I did all the flash stuff on the records..."

Although a fine pianist and singer, Vee never was comfortable performing in front of audiences and so she naturally fell into writing songs, penning a few early hits such as "**I'm Keepin' Company**" (with Lucy Bender Sokole and Dave Dreyer) and the plaintive "**I Couldn't Tell Them What to Do**" (with Roy Turk).

Yet the partnership of Seymour and Lawnhurst, formed in early 1935, brought

forth song after song that dominated the Hit Parade. Vee's bouncy, catchy style fit wonderfully with Tot's clever lyrics filled with phrases of the day. **"And Then Some,"** recorded by Ozzie Nelson, Bob Crosby and Joe Reichman, was on the Hit Parade for 11 weeks, **"Cross Patch"** was a big hit for Louis Prima (6 weeks on the Hit Parade), and Fats Waller did very well with the jaunty **"Us on a Bus,"** as did Rudy Vallee. Mr. Vallee also scored with **"What's the Name of That Song?"** The sprightly **"No Other One"** was recorded by Bob Crosby, Putney Dandridge and Little Jack Little, and stayed on the Hit Parade for 11 weeks. **"Accent on Youth,"** the title song of a film featuring Herbert Marshall, was recorded by a number of Big Bands, including the Duke Ellington Orchestra,

featuring Johnny Hodges. **"Please Keep Me in Your Dreams"** was recorded in 1936 by Billie Holliday.

From 1937 to 1944 Tot and Vee also contributed to a number of *Popeye the Sailor Man* cartoons, (but not the famous theme song, which was written by Sammy Lerner and Sammy Timberg) including the two-reel animated feature *Popeye the Sailor meets Ali Baba's Forty Thieves*.

Tot Seymour passed away in 1966. Vee Lawnhurst lived to be 87. As pianist and music historian Peter Mintun writes: *"she... eventually vanished from the public eye, enjoying her retirement in her Manhattan apartment with her Mason & Hamlin piano and happy memories."*

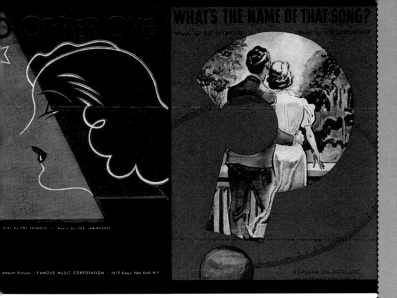

Tot Seymour
(LYRICS)

Vee Lawnhurst
(MUSIC)

e first successful team of girl song writers in the history of
ular music publishing. They were brought together in the
ing of 1935 and their first efforts resulted in the popular hit songs:

**"AND THEN SOME", "REVELATION",
"ACCENT ON YOUTH", "NO OTHER ONE"**

They were awarded a long term contract by Famous
Music Corp.— and give promise of continued success.

SELECTED SONGLIST...

- AND THEN SOME
- US ON A BUS
- WHAT'S THE NAME OF THAT SONG
- NO OTHER ONE
- ACCENT ON YOUTH
- PLEASE KEEP ME IN YOUR DREAMS

CONTRIBUTED TO:

- POPEYE THE SAILOR MAN CARTOON SERIES
- ABOU BEN BOOGIE

SUGGESTED LISTENING...

Crosspatch – Louis Prima

Us on a Bus – Fats Waller

Accent on Youth – Dinah Washington

SOURCES...

The Unsung Songwriters, Warren W. Vache,
Rowman and Littlefield Publishers, Inc., 2000

Peter Mintun, 2009, *Vee Lawnhurst*, Retrieved
January 2010, from http://www.imdb.com/name/
nm0492586/bio

Hodges, Frederick and Mintun, Peter. "Vee
Lawnhurst, Musical Star." **Musical Instrument
Collectors Association (AMICA)**, Volume 23,
Number 7 September-October, 1986.

Tot Seymour, Notable Songwriters, Retrieved
May 2009, from Songwriter's Hall of Fame,
http://www.songwritershalloffame.org/notable_
writers/C5037

DeLuxe
REPRODUCING PLAYER ROLL
Y-6995 $1.25
The Only Only One
Monaco & Warren
Fox-Trot
Played by
VEE LAWNHURST
© 1924 by Shapiro, Bernstein & Co.
Made in U. S. A.

CROSS PATCH
Words by TOT SEYMOUR   Music by VEE LAWNHURST

Publishers to Paramount Pictures • FAMOUS MUSIC CORP • *1619 Broadway, New York, N. Y.*

CBS PHOTO - RELEASED 10/28/36.
HALLOWE'EN'S HERE! says Vee Lawnhurst, song composer,
heard over the WABC-Columbia network with the Charioteers.

You've   just got to stay with me
I've   just got-ta fall for you

Pet me a lit-tle bit,   I doub-le dare you,   You're   doub-le O - kay
And when it comes to love   I'll hand it to   you,   Oh   ba - by you're there

Symbols for Guitar

LIL HARDIN ARMSTRONG

1902 – 1971

First Lady of Jazz

It's easy to overlook a musician who usually ends up being a footnote in someone else's biography. Lil Hardin Armstrong has too long been identified only as the wife of Louis Armstrong, at best getting a little credit for her early guidance of his career. In fact, Lil was one of the first jazz pianists, the anchor of many groups in those crucible years of jazz, and she was not only Louis' friend and manager, she was one of his best songwriters and arrangers.

Like Alberta Hunter (with whom she later became friends), Lil grew up in the tough, sensational Beale Street section of Memphis. Her hard working, church-going mother, Dempsey, was terrified that her daughter would be as attracted to the world of prostitution and crime as she was to the thrilling "Satan's music" which poured out of that neighborhood. Longing to offer Lillian a better life, Dempsey encouraged her daughter's classical music studies and moved them both out of Memphis to Chicago.

Despite the beating Lil received after Dempsey discovered W. C. Handy's "**St. Louis Blues**" hidden in her daughter's room, Lil appeared at Jones Music Store for more of this 'new' sheet music. Frustrated by the song demonstrator (it was common practice to have a pianist in music stores to give a live sample of new songs), Lillian started to play the music herself. Her sight reading and strong playing led to her being hired as demonstrator, which she kept secret from her protective mother. Lil was soon the pride of the store, and everyone talked about "Hot Miss Lil" who dressed like a school girl, read music like a scholar (very unusual in those circles) and played with outstanding rhythm and feeling.

One day Jelly Roll Morton stopped in and played a few songs - Lil Hardin said that she was knocked out by how rhythmic and loud his playing was, and determined to learn how

to play like that. Her big chance came when she was asked to join the Creole Jazz Band.

It was months before Dempsey found out, and she was apoplectic when she did. As recounted in James L. Dickerson's excellent biography, Lil stood her ground. Without music, the job opportunities for a black woman in Chicago were housekeeper and cook, and Lil pleaded with her mother to let her take her shot. Dempsey had always hoped to elevate her daughter beyond what she herself had settled for, and so she finally relented. But Dempsey made sure to show up every night at the nightclub to take Lil home.

By 1923, the band had become King Oliver's Creole Jazz Band, and was the hottest band in Chicago. Lil's contribution to every band she played in was her approach to the piano as an ensemble, rhythmic instrument. She'd lay down that 4/4 time so thick that even the tuba would swing, and wove a background designed to allow the other players in the band the best possible template over which they'd freely improvise.

Joe Oliver wanted to add a strong second trumpet, so he brought up a young man he knew from his New Orleans days, by the name of Louis Armstrong. When Lil met Louis she couldn't believe her eyes. "I didn't like the way he dressed and didn't like the way he talked," she reported. "He was a hick from the swamp." But when he played, even as 2nd trumpet, Lil noticed that people jammed the already crowded Dreamland Café, even white folks, who hung from the rafters to hear Louis Armstrong. And Louis was entirely smitten with her — a young refined lady, who loved jazz just as much as he did, so different from the rough women he'd known back home.

By both of their accounts, Lil "worked" on Louis; and he was her eager pupil. Working together each night in the hottest jazz band

THE BEST OF LOUIS ARMSTRONG: THE HOT FIVE AND HOT SEVEN RECORDINGS

Lil, 1933, Bandleade

Lil and Lo

of the time, they were also inseparable by day. They practiced classical music together, Lil insisting that Louis really learn to read and understand theory beyond what his ear told him, and she groomed him and bought him a new wardrobe. Superstars of their era, they were the pride of African American community in Chicago. Soon they were married and became known as the First Couple of Jazz.

Lil convinced Louis to leave Joe Oliver, and booked him under his own name. Louis often said he would never have left Oliver if Lil hadn't pushed him into it. In a taped interview with Chris Albertson years later, Lil ruefully laughed and said the musicians called Louis "Henny" because she hen-pecked him so much. In 1925, Lil set up, played on, and provided much original material for the Hot Five recording date on the Okeh label, universally regarded as the first true jazz session ever recorded, stepping away from Dixieland into a new art form.

Lil understood the value of copyrighting and recording original material, and made sure that the sessions featured plenty of originals. Many of her own pieces "**Struttin' with Some Barbeque**," "**King of the Zulus**," and "**I'm Gonna Gitcha**," were composed specifically to feature her talented husband. In "**I'm Gonna Gitcha**," the song begins with Louis' clear, powerful opening notes, followed by solo sections which are wrapped around composed breaks (which she carefully notated, unusual for that era) and ending with the sweet and gruff vocal that was to become synonymous with the name Louis Armstrong.

Sadly, the marriage did not last. Louis was fairly open about his other romantic involvements, which led him to maintain separate households, yet was loath to part with the one woman who always understood his music to the core. Aligning himself with crude and dishonest managers, he would return to Lil for occasional guidance. But eventually he turned his back on their long relationship. He was her heartache, and remained the true love of her life.

Lil returned to her own musical career in the 30's, forming two all-female bands (including Fletcher Henderson's wife Leora Mieux on trombone and Hazel Scott's mother Alma on clarinet and sax). Lil Hardin Armstrong and Her Swing Orchestra recorded many sides at Decca, featuring some of Lil's originals: "**My Secret Flame**," and "**Just for a Thrill**," in particular, reflect her grief at losing Louis.

She also opened a restaurant in Chicago ('Lil Armstrong's Swing Shack') serving soul food, and tried her hand at being a clothes designer.

Over the next few decades Lil toured in Europe and sporadically recorded and appeared in the States. Ray Charles' 1959 version of her song "**Just for a Thrill**" re-awakened the public's interest in her music and she was featured on Chris Albertson's **Living Legends** recordings (a series which also included Ida Cox and Alberta Hunter).

In 1971 the death of Louis Armstrong simply shattered Lillian. Seven weeks later she was asked to perform at a memorial concert for him. Performing "**St. Louis Blues**," she died onstage as she played the final chords of the song which had defined her in so many ways.

King Olliver's Creole Jazz Band

The Hot Five

SELECTED SONGLIST...

- STRUTTIN' WITH SOME BARBEQUE
- I'M GONNA GITCHA
- KING OF THE ZULUS
- MY HEART
- JUST FOR A THRILL
- MY SECRET FLAME
- SATCHEL MOUTH SWING
- HOTTER THAN THAT

SUGGESTED LISTENING...

Chicago: The Living Legends: Lil Hardin Armstrong – Riverside Label, 1961

Complete Hot Five and Hot Seven Recordings (box set with booklet) – Sony Music, 2008

"Just for a Thrill" – The Genius of Ray Charles – Atlantic Records, 1959

SOURCES...

Just For a Thrill: Lil Hardin Armstrong, First Lady of Jazz, James L. Dickerson, Cooper Square Press, 2002.

Louis Armstrong: An Extravagant Life, Laurence Bergreen, Broadway Books, 1997.

Stormy Weather: The Music and Lives of a Century of Jazzwomen, Linda Dahl, Pantheon Books, 1984

Albertson, Chris, *An Audio Interview with Lil Hardin Armstrong, part 1*, Retrieved September 2011, http://stomp-off.blogspot.com/2010/08/lil-armstrong-interview-1-of-2.html

Taylor, J. (2008) With Lovie and Lil: Rediscovering Two Chicago Pianists of the 1920's. *Big Ears, Listening for Gender in Jazz Studies*, Nichole T Rustin, Sherrie Tucker, (Eds), Duke University Press, 2008.

IDA COX

1886 - 1967

Uncrowned Queen of the Blues

With intelligence, sharp edged wit and clarion voice, singer-songwriter Ida Cox did more than just sing and write the blues – she came to represent the new black woman of the 1920s, who had something to say about her lot in life. Songs like "**Chicago Monkey Man Blues**" and "**Wild Women (Don't Have the Blues)**" rang with a powerful self-determination that still feels fresh today. "**Pink Slip Blues**" expressed a working woman's woes, and "**Last Mile Blues**" spoke plainly about the shameful issue of lynching, an all too common occurrence at the time. Her original songs particularly spoke to black women who longed for dignity and respect in a white man's world.

Born Ida Prather in Taccoa, Georgia, she was the daughter of poor sharecroppers. When Ida began singing in her church choir, her voice, sure and to the point, caught everyone's attention – she was simply born to sing. Barely thirteen, she ran away to join the tent and minstrel shows so prevalent in the South. A gifted comedienne and mimic, she was often put on stage. This early stage experience served her well in years to come.

At fourteen, she landed her first professional singing job with F.S Wolcott's *Rabbit Foot Minstrel Revue*, which also launched the careers of Bessie Smith and Ida's idol, Ma Rainey. She graduated to the vaudeville circuit, and her beauty, strong stage presence and sharp-witted song writing helped her become one of the favorite acts in the TOBA (Theatre Owners Booking Association) circuit.

In 1920, she formed, managed and produced her own traveling vaudeville troupe, *Raisin' Cain*, which proved to be so popular it became the first show associated with TOBA to open at the famed Apollo Theater in New York.

Still it was her direct, sure singing style that caught the ear of Paramount Records talent scout J. Mayo Williams, a colorful character in the earliest days of recording. After the tremendous success of Mamie Smith's 1920 release of "**Crazy Blues**," it was clear there was a big market for 'race records.' Williams went on the hunt for talent, but wanted to avoid the hugely popular Classic Blues singers, like Bessie Smith and Ma Rainey, whose live impact was often aided by elaborate stage sets, costuming and a flamboyant stage persona. It was pianist Lovie Austin who urged Williams to come hear Ida Cox, who was performing at the rundown Monogram Theatre at the time.

Ida's hard, clear voice and blunt cynical lyrics awed Williams. He described her as a woman who just "stood flat-footed and sang." Williams invited Ida and Lovie Austin to record at Paramount. Their first date resulted in "**Any Woman's Blues**," "**Bama Bound Blues**," and "**Lovin' is the Thing I'm Wild About**."

Paramount quickly became a major blues label with Ida Cox in the forefront. She was often billed as the "Sepia Mae West" or the "Uncrowned Queen of the Blues." From 1923 to 1929, Ida recorded 78 sides, mostly original songs, for Paramount as well as Broadway and Silverstone companies.

She also maintained a large vaudeville troupe during those years. Ida's tall, queenly bearing and beauty were greatly admired by audiences, and her steady, firm managerial habits helped her attract consistently fine performers, including Lovie Austin and her Blues Serenaders.

An ability to adapt to the times kept Ida working during the Depression, long after other Classic Blues singers of the 20's were forced to quit. She often performed at Café Society with her third husband, the excellent blues pianist Jesse Crump. The 1930's ended with an appearance at Carnegie Hall in John Hammond's *From Spirituals to Swing*, a series of concerts that brought mainstream recognition to African American music.

This concert earned Ida a new Jazz audience, and she was invited to record with Charlie Christian, Fletcher Henderson, and Lionel Hampton during the early 1940s. Sidelined by a stroke in 1945, Ida was living with her daughter in Tennessee, when journalist and record producer Chris Albertson coaxed her back into the studio in 1961. He recalled that she was hesitant to return to the studio after 21 years. She told Chris that she had read her own obituary in a trade magazine some years back and, "If they think I'm dead, I thought to myself, I might as well not disappoint them." Finally, Ida agreed to come up north and record "a final statement," which resulted in the powerful LP **Blues From Rampart Street**. She passed away in 1967 and was buried in Knoxville, Tennessee.

Ida Cox blazed the trail for many blues singers and had a particular influence on Koko Taylor, Etta James, and Tina Turner. She was a pioneer, a new model for black women of the time, and frankly, a role model for all women. She carried herself in such a manner that even when she sang the off-color lyrics of her vaudeville-influenced songs, she was perceived as no less a lady, no less the Queen of the Blues.

SOURCES...

Bessie, Chris Albertson, Stein & Day, 1972

Blues Singers: Biographies of 50 Legendary Artists of the Early 20th Century, David Dicaire, McFarland & Company Publishers, Inc., 1999

Spreadin' Rhythm Around: Black Popular Songwriters, 1880-1930, David A.Jasen, Gordon Gene Jones, Routledge Press, 2005

Nothing But the Blues: The Music and the Musicians, Edited by Lawrence Cohn, Abbeville Publishing Group, New York, 1993

Blues Legacies and Black Feminism: Gertrude "Ma" Rainey, Bessie Smith, and Billie Holiday, Angela Y. Davis, Pantheon Press, 1998

Albertson, Chris, *When Miss Ida Came To Town*, Retrieved April 1, 2011, from http://stomp-off.blogspot.com/2009/08/when-miss-ida-came-to-town.html

Ida Cox, Blues Woman of the Times, *African American Registry*, Retrieved November, 2009, from http://www.aaregistry.org/historic_events/view/ida-cox-blues-woman-times

SELECTED SONGLIST...

- 'BAMA BOUND BLUES
- PINK SLIP BLUES
- LAST MILE BLUES
- FOUR DAY CREEP
- WILD WOMEN (DON'T HAVE THE BLUES)
- CHICAGO MONKEY MAN BLUES
- ONE HOUR WOMAN
- HANDY MAN
- HOW LONG DADDY?
- DEATH LETTER BLUES
- TREE TOP TALL PAPA

SUGGESTED LISTENING...

"Blues For Rampart Street: Ida Cox with the Coleman Hawkins Quintet" (with Roy Eldridge, Sammy Price, Milt Hinton, Jo Jones) Concord Jazz Label, 1961. Recorded late in her life, what she's lost in terms of range is more than made up by her spirit.

"From Spirituals to Swing: 1938 & 1939 Carnegie Hall Concerts." Re-mastered 1999 with 2 tracks from Ms. Cox, this disc is a must-have for jazz and blues fans everywhere.

"Ida Cox: Complete Recorded Works, Vol. 4, 1927-1938" import, Document Records

THEATRE OWNERS BOOKING ASSOCIATION
CHATTANOOGA OFFICE: 1212-1213 VOLUNTEER BUILDING
SAM E. REEVIN, MANAGER

BOOKINGS

Date March 9th, 1928.   192

To Mr. Ben Stein,

Douglass   Theatre   Macon   City   Ga.   State

3 days   Week of APRIL 9th – 10th – 11th 1928

Name of Act	Salary	Commission	Address for Tickets
Ida Cox & Piano Accompanist	$50%	5%	Eighty-One Theatre, Atlanta, Ga.
Dick and Dick			
Ed Pete –			
Johnson and Johnson			
Miss Tressie Legge			
TOTAL	$50%	5%	

Remarks:

WILD WOMEN

Don't Have the Blues

IDA COX

FOREMOTHERS
Volume I

with the
COLEMAN HAWKINS Quintet

featuring
ROY ELDRIDGE

and

SAMMY PRICE
MILT HINTON
JO JONES

Ida Cox with Chris Albertson in recording studio.

Pamela Rose is a San Francisco based vocalist, songwriter and educator who has thrilled audiences locally and internationally with her swinging, soulful style.

Pamela believes her fascination with songwriters came from two streams: hearing her mother hum and sing standards night and day, and the lucky coincidence of being raised a block from the Troubadour, the West Hollywood nightclub that was to become a mecca for the emerging singer-songwriter scene of the early 1970's. "I poured all my teen angst into my songs, trotting them out on every amateur night stage I could find. The difficult, creative path to a well-written song has always intrigued me."

After graduating from U.C. Berkeley with a degree in 19th century literature, Pamela paid her dues singing in local coffee shops and bars until Hammond B-3 organist Merl Saunders recruited her for an East Coast Tour in 1977. Watching road veteran Saunders light up audiences every night taught the young singer a thing or two about the special relationship between performer and listener.

Over the next many years Rose was a mainstay in the Bay Area club scene, fronting original bands and touring with the Motown dance band, Zasu Pitts Memorial Orchestra. An increasing fascination with the well-crafted jazz standards her mother used to sing led Rose to record four albums and tour in Germany and Denmark, in addition to appearing at festivals and clubs on the West Coast.

In 2009 Pamela Rose recorded *Wild Women of Song: Great Gal Composers of the Jazz Era* at Skywalker Sound, with multiple Grammy™ award winner Leslie Ann Jones as producer and engineer. This highly regarded work sparked an entirely new chapter in Rose's career, as she researched and mounted a travelling multi-media theatrical concert which has played in London, Los Angeles and New York and the Bay Area. Rose combined elements of storytelling, archival photos and a live jazz performance to bring the tales of these fascinating, forgotten songwriters back to life. "I love getting a chance to not only honor these women – but also to remind audiences of this extraordinary era in American Music."

Pamela Rose is married to Steven Dinkelspiel, who puts up with her crazy schedule and has always appreciated Wild Women. They have two fabulous children Emma and Eli, who keep them humble and on their toes.

Rose is on the faculty of the Jazz School in Berkeley, and continues to sing jazz and blues in clubs and festivals everywhere.

THANK YOU...

It has been a wonderful experience to follow the trail back to the women heralded in this book. I have loved working on the project, and am so grateful to all the friends, colleagues and relatives who never hesitated to pitch in when they received my call. Of special note: Jennifer Melnick, my graphic artist whose striking images on screen and within these pages helped create magic. My editors, daughter Emma Dinkelspiel and sister in law Frances Dinkelspiel, photo archivist Farrol Mertes, dramaturg and cheerleader Jayne Wenger, Adam Hirschfelder and The Koret Foundation, whose early confidence in the project was so helpful. Harold Jacobs generously gave me so many rare and beautiful images and Peter Mintun was a fount of important information. Gayle Wilhelm, who pitched in every and any where help was needed. And unending gratitude to my dear husband and children who cheerfully gave up all hopes of creature comforts at home during the past year.

1) **WILD WOMEN (Don't Have the Blues)**
(4:08) Ida Cox
Universal Music Corporation

Matt Catingub (horn arr), Doug Beavers (trombone), Mike Olmos (trumpet), Matt Catingub (alto & tenor saxophones), Wayne De La Cruz (Hammond B-3 organ), Danny Caron (guitar) Dewayne Pate (bass), Dave Rokeach (drums)

2) **I DON'T KNOW ENOUGH ABOUT YOU**
(3:09) Peggy Lee, Dave Barbour
Denslow Music Inc.

Matt Catingub (arr), Matt Catingub (piano, alto saxophone), Ruth Davies (bass), Jason Lewis (drums)

3) **A FINE ROMANCE** (3:29)
Dorothy Fields, Jerome Kern,
Aldi Music Company

Matt Catingub (arr), Doug Beavers (trombone), Mike Olmos (trumpet), Matt Catingub (alto & tenor saxophones, piano), Danny Caron (guitar), Ruth Davies (bass), Dave Rokeach (drums)

4) **DOWN HEARTED BLUES** (5:53)
Alberta Hunter, Lovie Austin
Alberta Hunter Music

Tammy Hall (piano), Danny Caron (guitar), Ruth Davies (bass), Allison Miller (drums)

5) **THAT OLE DEVIL CALLED LOVE** (5:08)
Allan Roberts, Doris Fisher
Universal Music Corporation,
Roberts Allan Music Co.

John R. Burr (arr), John R. Burr (piano), Jeff Massanari (guitar), Jim Zimmerman (vibes), Jon Evans (bass), Jason Lewis (drums)

6) **CAN'T WE BE FRIENDS?** (3:33)
Kay Swift, Paul James
Warner Bros Inc.

Matt Catingub (arr), Mike Olmos (trumpet), Matt Catingub (piano, alto saxophone), Danny Caron (guitar), Ruth Davies (bass), Jason Lewis (drums)

7) **I'M NOT MISSING YOU** (5:00)
Pamela Rose, Danny Caron,
Wayne De La Cruz
Prosesong Publishing

Wayne De La Cruz (arr), Joe Cohen (tenor saxophone), Wayne De La Cruz (Hammond B-3 organ), Danny Caron (guitar), Allison Miller (drums), Jordan Koppelman, Linda Tillery, Jeanie Tracey, Glenn Walters (bg vocals)

8) **WHAT A DIFF'RENCE A DAY MADE** (4:43)
Stanley Adams, Maria Grever
Universal Music Z-Tunes, LLC, Stanley Adams Music

Tammy Hall (piano), Ruth Davies (bass), Allison Miller (drums)

9) **CLOSE YOUR EYES** (5:00)
Bernice Petkere
Bernice Petkere Music Company

Mimi Fox (guitar), Wayne De La Cruz (Hammond B-3 organ), Jon Evans (bass), Allison Miller (drums)

10) **AND THEN SOME** (4:30)
Tot Seymour, Vee Lawnhurst
Music Sales Corp

John R. Burr (arr), John R. Burr (piano), Jon Evans (bass), Jason Lewis (drums)

11) **JUST FOR A THRILL** (4:58)
Lil Hardin Armstrong, D. Raye
Louis Armstrong Music, MCA

Danny Caron (guitar), Tony Stead (Hammond B-3 organ), Bryant Mills (drums)

12) **IT'S A GOOD DAY** (3:36)
Peggy Lee, Dave Barbour
Denslow Music Inc.

John R. Burr (arr), John R. Burr (piano), Carl Wheeler (Hammond B-3 organ), Jon Evans (bass), Jason Lewis (drums), Linda Tillery (voc arr), Linda Tillery, Jeanie Tracey, Glenn Walters (bg vocals)

All tracks except # 7": Produced, Recorded and Mixed by Leslie Ann Jones at Skywalker Sound, a LucasFilm Ltd. Company, Marin County, CA Additional recording at Fantasy Studios, Berkeley and Broken Radio, San Francisco.

Just For a Thrill (Track #7): Produced by Danny Caron Engineered by Bruce Kaphan Recorded at Fantasy Studios and Bruce Kaphan Studios, Fremont, CA.

Additional mastering and sequencing by Judy Kirschner.